BUNBURY

A Serious Play for Trivial People

Tom Jacobson

D1240594

BROADWAY PLAY PUBLISHING INC
56 E 81st St., NY NY 10028-0202
212 772-8334 fax: 212 772-8358
BroadwayPlayPubl.com

BUNBURY
© Copyright 2008 by Tom Jacobson

First printing: May 2008
I S B N: 0-88145-388-9

Book design: Marie Donovan
Word processing: Microsoft Word
Typographic controls: Ventura Publisher
Typeface: Palatino
Printed and bound in the U S A

ABOUT THE AUTHOR

Tom Jacobson is a playwright who has had more than fifty productions in Los Angeles and around the country, including SPERM at Circle X Theater Company, THE ORANGE GROVE at Playwrights Arena, and the award-winning BUNBURY, TAINTED BLOOD and OUROBOROS at The Road Theater Company. He is a co-literary manager of The Theater @ Boston Court, a founding member of Playwrights Ink, and a board member of Cornerstone Theater Company. He teaches playwriting and related courses for U C L A Extension. Upcoming productions include world premieres of THE CHINESE MASSACRE (ANNOTATED) at Circle X and THE FRIENDLY HOUR at The Road Theater Company.

BUNBURY was produced by The Road Theater Company in Los Angeles (Julie Quinn and Kimberly Valkenaar, Producers; Taylor Gilbert, Executive Producer), opening on 30 September 2005. The cast and creative contributors were as follows:

LADY BRACKNELL/OLGA/MARTHA/
OLD CECILY .... Peggy Billo
HARTLEY/ROMEO/VLADIMIR ....Scot Burklin
FRIAR LAWRENCE/LAWYER/
GEORGE/OLD ALGERNON .... Michael Dempsey
ALGERNON/ALLAN/JIM .... Zach Dulli
ROSALINE/GWENDOLEN/MASHA ....Ann Noble
JACK/ESTRAGON .... Steve Reisberg
JULIET/CECILY/IRINA/BLANCHE ....Stephanie Stearns
BUNBURY ....Sean Wing

Understudies: .... Don Grigware, Liz Herron,
Shannon Morris, Kimberly Valkenaar, John
Cragen, Quinn Hanchette, Ammar Mahmood

Director ....Mark Bringelson
Set design ....Sibyl Wickersheimer
Lighting design ....Henry M Sume
Costume design ....Samantha Wright
Sound design .... David B Marling
Assistant sound design .... Lee E Osteen II
Prop design .... Lila Waters
Resident vocal coach .... Linda de Vries
Fight choreographer .... Kelly Van Kirk
Master carpenter ....Derek Bjornson
Puppets .... Tony Urbano & Carl Johnson

Publicity & photography . . . . .Marci Hill
Graphic design . . . . .Jeff Griffith
Stage managers . . . . .Greg Baker & Matt Kaiser
Assistant stage manager . . . . Bettina Zacar

CHARACTERS

BUNBURY, *twenties*
HARTLEY, *twenties*
ROSALINE, *twenties*
JACK, *twenties*
ALGERNON, *twenties*
ROMEO, *twenties*
JULIET, *mid teens*
FRIAR LAWRENCE, *fifties*
LADY BRACKNELL, *fifties*
CECILY CARDEW, *twenties*
GWENDOLEN FAIRFAX, *twenties*
LAWYER, *fifties*
MASHA, *thirties*
OLGA, *thirties*
IRENA, *twenties*
ALLAN, *late teens*
BLANCHE, *late teens*
JIM, *twenty*
GEORGE, *forty-six*
MARTHA, *fifty-two*
VLADIMIR, *twenties*
ESTRAGON, *twenties*
OLD ALGERNON, *ninety-six*
OLD CECILY, *ninety-four*

The play can be performed by five men and three women.
All roles except BUNBURY *may be doubled, tripled or*
quadrupled as follows:

ROSALINE/GWENDOLEN/MASHA
FRIAR LAWRENCE/LAWYER/GEORGE/OLD ALGERNON
JACK/ESTRAGON
HARTLEY/ROMEO/VLADIMIR
ALGERNON/ALLAN/JIM
LADY BRACKNELL/OLGA/MARTHA/OLD CECILY
CECILY/BLANCHE/JULIET/IRENA

SETTING

The action takes place in various locations across several eras, including a drawing room and country garden in Victorian England; a tomb in Medieval Verona; a Baltimore study in 1830; a 1903 sitting room in provincial Russia; a park, train compartment and bedroom in 1930s Mississippi; the living room of a house on the campus of a small New England college in 1962; a timeless country road; and a study in 1969 London.

Simple chairs and tables, with lighting creating the changing locations.

(The morning room of an English country home, circa 1895.
BUNBURY *sits, reading, with glass of wine. He is a very
attractive young man in his twenties, wearing stylish
"at home" clothes of the Victorian era.* HARTLEY, *twenties,
brings him a plate of sandwiches.)*

BUNBURY: No, thank you, Hartley, I'm reading.

HARTLEY: It is well past noon, sir.

BUNBURY: If literature be the food of love, read on!

HARTLEY: A gross paraphrase, sir.

BUNBURY: It is not a paraphrase. It is an epigram.

HARTLEY: Albeit a poor one, sir. *(Helps himself to a
sandwich)*

BUNBURY: Man doth not live by bread alone.

HARTLEY: *(His mouth full)* An accurate quote, sir,
but blasphemous out of context. I observe you are
remarkably allusive this afternoon.

BUNBURY: I am always allusive. Original thinking does
not exist, and attempts at originality merely waste time.
Everything has been said before, and need only be
rearranged to suit the occasion. It is merely a matter
of knowing what to quote when. Are you educated,
Hartley?

HARTLEY: No, sir. I went to English schools.

BUNBURY: *(Holding up his book)* Have you read *Romeo
and Juliet*? Or seen it staged?

HARTLEY: *(Having another sandwich)* I object to comedy. It is morally instructive.

BUNBURY: It is a tragedy.

HARTLEY: I have only heard the symphony, sir, by Berlioz, and found it distressingly optimistic. The lovers die at the height of their passion, never experiencing the tedium of eternal love.

BUNBURY: Have you never fallen in love, Hartley?

HARTLEY: No, sir. It seemed precipitous.

BUNBURY: Everybody should have one great love!

HARTLEY: In literature, perhaps. In life, one should fall in love many times or not at all.

BUNBURY: That is very modern thinking, Hartley, and certainly immoral.

HARTLEY: But practical, sir. Romeo was on the path to a happy life—a charming parade of unrequited passions—when he lost his way with Juliet.

BUNBURY: What you are saying is highly offensive and refreshingly original. Do you suggest he would have been happier with Rosaline?

HARTLEY: *(Taking another sandwich)* Had he continued mooning after the chaste and virginal Rosaline, he'd be alive today, not lying poisoned on the floor of a Veronese tomb.

BUNBURY: He would *not* be alive. He is fictional. And please stop eating my sandwiches. What kind are they?

HARTLEY: Watercress, sir. And uncommonly dry. *(Drinks of BUNBURY's wine)*

BUNBURY: I find your speculation on the virginity of Rosaline somewhat alarming. It bespeaks an emotional life inappropriate to your class.

HARTLEY: It is supported by the text, sir.

BUNBURY: She is a minor character. She does not even appear!

HARTLEY: Through no fault of her own, sir.

BUNBURY: Certainly she could have made an appearance had she been paying proper attention.

HARTLEY: It is indeed calculation, sir.

BUNBURY: On the author's part, you mean?

HARTLEY: Exactly, sir. No actress ever brings her beauty down to earth, sullies it with corporeal matter. The same cannot be said for Juliet, especially as played these days by actresses corporeal in excess. *(Takes another sandwich)*

BUNBURY: Good heavens, Hartley! You are a secret dualist! A Manichean!

HARTLEY: She lives only in my imagination.

BUNBURY: You are in love after all!

HARTLEY: But unrequited, sir.

BUNBURY: Of course, Hartley, one can't expect a fictional character to return one's affection with equal ardor. What am I saying? She is less than fiction. She's sub-fictional!

HARTLEY: But she is mine.

BUNBURY: When Mister Moncrieff returns from London, I shall seek his advice about your continued employment in this house. You have populated it with imaginary and fantastical young ladies of questionable morals—I feel soiled.

HARTLEY: She is a virgin. A nun!

BUNBURY: You go too far, Hartley. Romeo says she refuses to "stay the siege of loving terms," not that she cloistered herself. Perhaps she is a lesbian.

HARTLEY: I do not believe in lesbians, sir. I am a Victorian.

BUNBURY: I merely offer an alternative reading. Had Romeo been in love with a religious it would have been remarked upon.

HARTLEY: "She hath sworn that she will still live chaste."

BUNBURY: You *have* read the play! You are not to be trusted around young and impressionable persons!

HARTLEY: It is only literature, sir.

BUNBURY: But you have used it to conjure lewd, living images! Made it far too personal, given it flesh. Art is to enlighten and elevate, not titillate!

HARTLEY: Not breathe?

BUNBURY: Literature is precious and unchanging, like a Japanese print in a museum. Preserved under glass for future generations, it is eternal. You've smeared the play with your intimate thoughts. I can't possibly read it again. I'm afraid I shall have to ask you to—

(A bell rings.)

BUNBURY: —To—to answer the door.

(HARTLEY leaves.)

BUNBURY: How extraordinary! Hartley is clearly derelict in his duties, cultivating instead a literary taste that borders on the lascivious. Prying into the virginity of an entirely fictitious character, moreover one who never puts in an appearance! Just wait till Algy returns!

HARTLEY: *(Appearing.)* A young lady to see you, sir.

BUNBURY: I'm expecting no one.

HARTLEY: In Renaissance costume, sir.

BUNBURY: If she is soliciting for a charity, please give her tuppence then send her on her way.

HARTLEY: Speaking iambic pentameter, sir.

BUNBURY: Next you will say she's using the archaic form of the intimate pronoun!

HARTLEY: I have not had occasion to exchange intimate pronouns with her, sir.

BUNBURY: What does this antiquated and rhythmic young person want with me?

HARTLEY: She seems affronted, sir. And quite insistent.

BUNBURY: (*Motioning assent.* HARTLEY *leaves.*) Modern life is full of such assaults. One can't go anywhere without being pummeled by poetry or vilified in verse. Even music is a weapon nowadays. Berlioz indeed!

(ROSALINE *comes in wearing an Italian Renaissance gown. She is a beautiful woman in her twenties.*)

BUNBURY: Good afternoon. You must be new to the neighborhood. Few young ladies of Woolton wear farthingales when making calls these days.

ROSALINE: Art thou the wretch dares slander my fair name?

BUNBURY: I very greatly doubt it, as I don't know your name, fair or not.

ROSALINE: I am called Rosaline. And thy name, sir?

BUNBURY: Edgar Bunbury, of the Shropshire Bunburys.

(ROSALINE *laughs.*)

BUNBURY: My name amuses you? *I'm* the one who should be laughing. In fact, I will! Ha ha!

ROSALINE: 'Tis trivial. What's in a name? In thine
There's all the substance of a light dessert.

BUNBURY: Now you've really tipped your hand!
My friend Algernon accuses me of triviality—
his very word! You're another of his jokes, with
your panto costume and your versification.
Obviously, Hartley is in on it as well.

ROSALINE: 'Twere not for you, I shan't have come at all.
A maiden lady's name is all she hath,
And stealing mine doth not thy treasure prove
But makes me that much poorer just the same.

BUNBURY: And Hartley chided me for paraphrase!
You're quoting from Othello now, I think,
But not adhering closely to the text.
I can't imagine how this could get worse—
Good heavens! Now you've got me spouting verse!

ROSALINE: And rhyming couplets, too!

BUNBURY: Let's stop right now. I will not risk another
word.

ROSALINE: But how—?

(BUNBURY *cuts her off with a gesture.*)

BUNBURY: *(Carefully)* You claim you're Rosaline?

ROSALINE: Indeed, that's so.

BUNBURY: From Shakespeare's play?

ROSALINE: I'm from Verona.

BUNBURY: No!

ROSALINE: 'Tis true.

BUNBURY: Then speak Italian if you can.

ROSALINE: That's what we're speaking now—

BUNBURY: When we began
You spoke in verse with many thous and thees.
You've made me rhyme as quickly as you please.
We each affect the other—

ROSALINE: What a state!

BUNBURY: I versify—you've grown more up to date!

HARTLEY: *(Entering)* Some prose, sir?

BUNBURY: Yes, we rhyme against our will—

ROSALINE: And find that every iamb we fulfill—

HARTLEY: I suspect a dense paragraph of spondees, dactyls and trochees thoughtfully jammed together will handily solve your dilemma. Multisyllabic words of Latin origin also mitigate the headlong rush of Anglo Saxon rhythm. Poetry can be contagious, and has been carefully regulated throughout history for that very reason. Any number of lives, loves, and important military campaigns have been lost through careless deployment of verse. *(Pause)* Will that be sufficient, sir?

BUNBURY: Yes, I think so, Hartley. Thank you.

HARTLEY: Very good, sir. *(Leaves)*

BUNBURY: You realize, of course, we are not speaking Italian, but English.

ROSALINE: I don't know English.

BUNBURY: Algy has no money whatsoever. I am astonished he would spend what little he has on this elaborate and hastily conceived practical joke. How much has he paid you? I hope you were not foolish enough to take credit.

ROSALINE: By algae do you mean pond scum?

BUNBURY: Some might say so, yes. But he's a generous and thoughtful gentleman, if occasionally given to absurd pranks. In fact, he has only just left for London to minister to a frightfully chronic invalid named Ernest.

ROSALINE: I know him not.

BUNBURY: Come, come. You are found out! An actress Algy's directed to impersonate the mysterious Rosaline from Shakespeare's *Tragedy of Romeo and Juliet.*

ROSALINE: Romeo!

BUNBURY: You've heard of him at least?

ROSALINE: And Juliet? My cousin?

BUNBURY: His star-crossed love.

ROSALINE: The little bitch!

BUNBURY: Now, now, she's nothing of the sort.
An innocent swept up in the tragic feud between the Capulets and Montagues.

ROSALINE: Obviously, you know her not. And Romeo—what hath she to do with him?

BUNBURY: She kills herself for him and he for her.

ROSALINE: They killed themselves? When?

BUNBURY: Continually, every time the play is staged. You don't know this? Even my butler studied Shakespeare in school.

ROSALINE: What is Shakespeare? A military maneuver?

BUNBURY: Very nearly. A playwright.

ROSALINE: A bellicose playwright wrote about my cousin and—and—? *(Weeps)*

BUNBURY: You're in it, too! Well, not you, of course, but the young lady you are pretending to be. What, crocodile tears?

ROSALINE: Romeo is dead!

BUNBURY: Now you've truly strayed from the script. Rosaline cared not a fig for Romeo.

ROSALINE: So he believed. A maiden hides her heart e'en as she gives it. Especially a maid who's merely pretty, not a beauty.

BUNBURY: What utter nonsense—you're quite beautiful. And as you are an actress, you're certainly well aware of the fact.

ROSALINE: But not so lovely as my cousin. Not fair enough for Romeo.

BUNBURY: *(Showing her the play)* If it gives you any comfort, here's what he says about you.

ROSALINE: *(Reading)*
She is too fair, too wise, wisely too fair,
To merit bliss by making me despair.

BUNBURY: See? Your chastity is his despair.

ROSALINE: Why says he this, when he no longer cares for me?

BUNBURY: This is the beginning of the play, before he meets Juliet at the Capulet ball. They exchange a ravishing sonnet and a kiss—more than one, in fact—and then fate conspires to destroy them.

ROSALINE: *I* am destroyed!

BUNBURY: No, my dear, you never existed at all, except in Romeo's fulsome verse. You are an offstage character— *(Aside)* —Actors are forever trying to enlarge their roles! *(To* ROSALINE*)* You are a nonentity!

ROSALINE: *(Trying to regain her dignity)* And yet I stand before you. A woman ruined without ravishment, dishonored not deflowered. He knelt before me, wept his love upon my carpets, but I was cold. He scaled my wall at night—

BUNBURY: Yes, that sounds like him!

ROSALINE: —But I would not open my window.
And now, o fickle youth, his pent-up passion poured
out another way, and my young cousin drenches with
his love—

BUNBURY: My, that's vivid.

ROSALINE: Beware, Bunbury, of passion overspilling—
it melts and runs away!

BUNBURY: What has Romeo's frivolity to do with me?
It's only a play.

ROSALINE: Have you no passion in your life?

BUNBURY: If I did what business would it be of yours?
A phantom character? A few drops of ink, that's all
you are. What has literature to do with life?

ROSALINE: You could be abandoned as easily as I.

BUNBURY: Abandoned? Now you are Cassandra?
You're mixing styles and periods in a most unseemly
way. Where are the unities? Where is order?

ROSALINE: Where is your generous and thoughtful
friend Algy?

BUNBURY: True to character, he is visiting the sick.

ROSALINE: True to character?

BUNBURY: *(After a moment)* Hartley!

(HARTLEY *appears, perhaps too quickly.)*

BUNBURY: What route did Mister Moncreiff take to
London?

HARTLEY: The usual, sir.

BUNBURY: Might I catch him if I leave immediately?

HARTLEY: Indeed, sir. He is quite leisurely in his habits.

BUNBURY: Send the carriage round, please.

HARTLEY: He will be rather irritated, sir, to be followed.

BUNBURY: As am I at this moment. Off he runs to succor his invalid Ernest, leaving me to fend off hysteric actresses in period attire.

(HARTLEY *leaves.*)

BUNBURY: I'm sorry, miss, if I'm not amused by your charade. Algernon has never taken literature seriously, and intends to humiliate me with this maudlin parody of classic text.

ROSALINE: Dost depart?

BUNBURY: I dost!

ROSALINE: But what of me?

BUNBURY: Back to your touring company, I expect. Unless, of course, you are indeed fair Rosaline, in which case— *(Holds up the book)* —Jump like Alice back through the looking glass!

HARTLEY: The carriage, sir.

BUNBURY: Farewell, counterfeit ingènue.

(BUNBURY *leaves.* HARTLEY *remains, staring at* ROSALINE *in a way that makes her uncomfortable. Lights out on them and up on* JACK, *carrying a lily and lurking in a garden, perhaps in an arbor. He is a very attractive young man and seems to be preparing to make a dramatic entrance wearing deepest mourning, with crepe hatband and black gloves. He practices a convulsive sob or two.* BUNBURY *appears suddenly, looking more than a little suspicious.)*

JACK: *(Startled)* I say!

BUNBURY: Good heavens! An undertaker in the shrubbery!

JACK: You are mistaken, sir. I am not an undertaker, but a gentleman.

BUNBURY: What would a gentleman be doing in the bushes?

JACK: My very question! Are you a gentleman, sir?

BUNBURY: *(Affronted)* Quite so.

JACK: May I inquire, in that case, what you are doing in the bushes?

BUNBURY: I cannot see what business it is of yours.

JACK: They are my bushes.

BUNBURY: I had not realized it customary in this part of Shropshire to lurk amongst the briars wearing crepe.

JACK: *(Offering the lily as proof)* I am in mourning.

BUNBURY: In the bushes.

JACK: I am in mourning for my brother. He loved these bushes.

BUNBURY: I see.

JACK: The matter being settled, I am well within my rights to reiterate: what are you doing in my bushes?

BUNBURY: Upon occasion, while walking in the country, a gentleman may find himself in need of a certain privacy.

JACK: You have a private need.

BUNBURY: That is correct.

(They stare at each other for a long moment, hostile, but intrigued.)

BUNBURY: A *private* need.

JACK: My auditory faculties are quite intact, and your enunciation was without impediment the first time you mentioned your desire for privacy. Pray, leave me to my grief. It is profound.

BUNBURY: My dear mister—?

JACK: *(Reluctantly.)* Worthing.

BUNBURY: Mister Worthing, I hope I may be allowed to offer my sincerest apologies. Oftimes a need for privacy blinds one to others' equally immeasurable needs. What was your unfortunate brother's name?

JACK: *(Even more reluctantly)* Ernest.

BUNBURY: Ernest! My dear Mister Worthing, that explains it all! I cannot possibly convey the cloud you have lifted.

JACK: You are suddenly gleeful. At my brother's passing?

BUNBURY: Was he a long-time invalid?

JACK: *(Has to think about it)* Yes.

BUNBURY: And you are attired thus for his funeral here today?

JACK: *(Worried)* Yes.

BUNBURY: *(Embraces JACK)* Thank you so very much! My mind is greatly eased!

JACK: *(Made nervous by the embrace)* Forgive me if I do not share your cheer.

BUNBURY: *(Stepping back)* Of course, of course. My joy is private joy, as your grief is private grief. I must embrace you once again, this time to convey my deepest sympathies. *(Embraces JACK once more)* I, also, have no brother. I know exactly how you feel.

JACK: Did your brother also die tragically?

BUNBURY: *(Stepping back)* No, I am an only child. The grief you now experience, I have known for a lifetime.

JACK: *(After a moment while they stare at each other uncomfortably)* May I ask your name, sir?

BUNBURY: Bunbury.

JACK: What an astonishing coincidence!

BUNBURY: It is not a common name.

JACK: Indeed not! But you look in the pink of health, remarkably vigorous, so you are certainly not the same fellow.

BUNBURY: I have always been blessed with exceptional health, I am proud to say, although the accomplishment is hardly mine to boast of.

JACK: Perhaps he is a relative. Do you have any sickly relations?

BUNBURY: As I mentioned to you just now, I am an only child. And, in fact, I have no relatives at all that I am aware of.

JACK: *(Perking up)* Yet another coincidence! I also have no relations to speak of.

BUNBURY: Now that your brother has found his reward.

(They both look sad for a moment.)

BUNBURY: Is this debilitated Bunbury a friend of your bedridden brother? Often those types seek each others' company.

JACK: Oh, no, he is an...acquaintance...of my friend Algernon Moncreiff. If you can call him that.

BUNBURY: Whatever do you mean? What does this Mister Moncreiff say about his acquaintance Bunbury?

JACK: Perhaps even acquaintance is too strong a word. He is more of an excuse.

BUNBURY: An excuse for what?

JACK: Whenever Algy needs to get away from London, he tells everyone he must tend to the languishing Bunbury in the country. He calls it Bunburying.

BUNBURY: How very clever of him. Was Mister Moncrieff also acquainted with your late brother Ernest?

JACK: I should hope not! My brother was too ill to know anyone.

BUNBURY: It simply occurred to me how convenient for this frightfully inventive Mister Moncrieff to have a frequently relapsing friend Ernest in London and this poor excuse of an acquaintance Bunbury in the country similarly stricken.

JACK: Fortunately, as I have indicated, Algy and Ernest are unacquainted. *Were.*

(Again the hostile but heated mutual stare. BUNBURY *looks into the distance toward the house.)*

BUNBURY: My urgent desire has been postponed but not greatly eased by this conversation.

(They glare at each other.)

BUNBURY: What sort of gentleman are you, sir, who will not leave another to his privacy?

JACK: It is my privacy that is invaded, but as I am no bounder, I will turn my back for a moment. *(He does so, with great style.)*

BUNBURY: Very well. *(Begins fumbling with his trouser buttons)* But a true gentleman would also move out of earshot. *(Turns away also, and tries to urinate)*

JACK: Consider yourself fortunate that I do not call the county constable to report your trespass in my copse. Civility and even security having deteriorated in the modern world, one is naturally cautious about any gentleman encountered amongst ornamental plantings. *(Sneaking a peek)* Pardon me, but are you experiencing some distress?

BUNBURY: *(Turning toward* JACK, *then quickly away as* JACK *turns toward him.)* Whatever do you mean?

JACK: I detect a noticeable silence that gives the lie to your urgency.

BUNBURY: Pray honor me with your silence so I may concentrate.

JACK: What degree of concentration is required for an act that infants find largely involuntary, I cannot imagine. *(Sneaks a peek)* Oh, I see.

BUNBURY: *(Turning, almost catching him)* I beg your pardon?

JACK: Nothing.

(JACK sneaks another peek, but this time BUNBURY catches him. Their eyes meet and they do not look away. Suddenly ALGERNON, yet another handsome young man, appears.)

ALGERNON: *(Startled)* Bunbury!

BUNBURY & JACK: Algy!

(Startled, BUNBURY hastily does up his trousers.)

ALGERNON: Ernest!

(BUNBURY and JACK look at each other once more, in a panic, then JACK simply runs away.)

ALGERNON: Jack! Wherever are you going? Jack!

BUNBURY: Is his name Jack, or Ernest?

ALGERNON: Until just yesterday he was Ernest, but today he is Jack. Whatever are you doing here?

BUNBURY: I might ask you the same.

ALGERNON: You've followed me!

BUNBURY: You said you were off to London to visit your diseased friend, Ernest, whom—I understand from this gentleman of ambiguous nomenclature—has just died.

ALGERNON: Indeed. Once I realized it was too late to reach his deathbed, I returned to Shropshire.

BUNBURY: To offer comfort to the late Ernest's brother, Jack?

ALGERNON: Exactly! Funerals, as they say, are for the living. Jack appears to be taking it quite hard. I wonder where he has run off to.

BUNBURY: I imagine it must be especially wrenching when one's dead brother shares one's name, or at least did until yesterday.

ALGERNON: They were very close.

BUNBURY: Why would their parents christen them with the same name?

ALGERNON: I suspect it simplified child-rearing enormously. Ernest is a marvelous name, a distinguished, solid-sounding name, and eminently trustworthy. I am seriously considering it myself.

BUNBURY: Changing your name?

ALGERNON: To Ernest. Now that there is one less in the world, it should not matter if there is another.

BUNBURY: Whatever for? Algernon is a perfectly lovely name. I much prefer it. Ernest sounds far too... strenuous.

ALGERNON: Nevertheless, I am being rechristened.

BUNBURY: When?

ALGERNON: This afternoon. I was on the way to the rectory when I stumbled upon you and Ernest— I mean Jack—here in this grove deeply engaged in— what *were* you engaged in, if I may ask?

BUNBURY: Conversation. About you, as it turns out.

ALGERNON: Well, I wish you wouldn't. The only thing worse than being talked about is being talked about by two dandies on a grassy knoll in the middle of Shropshire.

BUNBURY: You are trying to confuse the matter by calling me a dandy. Why do you seek christening at this advanced age?

ALGERNON: It is complicated.

BUNBURY: No doubt.

ALGERNON: I am engaged to be married.

BUNBURY: *(After a tense moment)* Marriage is not in the least complicated. In fact, it is quite the simplest thing in the world. Now I understand everything, and will be leaving. *(Begins to step away.)*

ALGERNON: *(Catching his arm)* My dear Bunbury, you don't understand at all. Cecily's a lovely girl—of course that is very important—but more to the point she is especially well off. An heiress.

BUNBURY: Perhaps it is best you change your name, for clearly you are a different person than I have come to know.

ALGERNON: Nothing is different! Nothing need change! Only my level of anxiety about finances will subside, and everything will be ever so much more pleasant.

BUNBURY: Only when you go to London you will no longer minister to your hypochondriacal friend Ernest, but perform your conjugal duties.

ALGERNON: Exactly. Duties in both cases.

BUNBURY: Algy, I've met Ernest, and I suspect your duties to him afford you far more pleasure than pain.

ALGERNON: It's a different Ernest!

BUNBURY: There appear to be at least three, and I am developing rather a negative opinion of all of them. Rosaline was right.

ALGERNON: Who is Rosaline? I would rather not learn any more new names today.

BUNBURY: I should be pleased to tell you she is the woman to whom I have become engaged. It would serve you right. But in fact I am not engaged to anyone. Nor do I expect to be. Rosaline—as you know perfectly well—is the name of the young lady Romeo loved before he met Juliet, and the name assumed by the actress you sent me this morning to act that part.

ALGERNON: For heaven's sake, Bunbury, haven't I enough other complications on my mind? Why on earth would I ask someone to impersonate a Shakespearean character whom—as I recall—we never even see on stage?

BUNBURY: To distract me from your other complications, such as christening and impending marriage?

ALGERNON: I have never given Rosaline a second thought. She is a mere device, not even a character. She gives Romeo an opportunity to utter poetic clichés about love, with which Shakespeare later contrasts the overwhelming passion Romeo feels for Juliet. Rosaline means nothing.

BUNBURY: She means *something*. Everyone's life means something.

ALGERNON: She doesn't *have* a life! She is literature, which is nothing but decoration for life, and won't change the world one whit. You have an overactive imagination and dwell on trivial details. Now run on home, stop trespassing in Jack or Ernest's woods, and try living on earth for five minutes!

BUNBURY: Where are you going?

ALGERNON: To the rectory. When next you see me, please remember to call me Ernest. *(Starts to leave)*

BUNBURY: Algernon!

ALGERNON: *(Stopping, softening)* Bunbury, it will be all right. Trust me, this is how it's always been done. It's not our world—we only live in it as best we can. *(Kisses him rather passionately)*

ROSALINE: *(Appearing)* And now it seems I am a mere device!

BUNBURY: *(As he and* ALGERNON *quickly part)* Oh dear, she is so easily irritated!

*(*ALGERNON *runs away.)*

ROSALINE: Wast that thy Algernon?

*(*BUNBURY *shrugs as if to say "who else?")*

ROSALINE: He's fickle, too.

BUNBURY: Just as you said. Men seem to run away from me today.

ROSALINE: He doth not seem full worthy of thy love.

BUNBURY: At this very moment, I'm inclined to agree. But you've only seen him at his worst—he feigns aversion to literature because it's fashionable at present.

ROSALINE: 'Tis always the fashion.

BUNBURY: Was it he who paid you to perform this role?

ROSALINE: I am not an actress. I am a Capulet!

BUNBURY: Indeed, he also denied it.

ROSALINE: Thy heart is crushéd like a rose that ne'er Had chance to bloom.

BUNBURY: And now my petals have been bruised and strewed
About the room. (*Starts*) Dammit, we're rhyming again.

ROSALINE: Don't worry—it didn't really scan. Unless you count septameter. Is there such a thing?

BUNBURY: Septenary verse works well in Latin, but the line is too long for English—what am I saying? My petals are bruised and it makes me cross.

ROSALINE: As are mine. Might we be of help to one another? Come with me.

BUNBURY: You've done nothing but introduce confusion into a well-ordered life.

ROSALINE: I merely revealed deceptions 'neath the glaze of civility. Let our bruiséd buds be born beyond the black, benighted—

BUNBURY: It would be improper of me to accompany you anywhere unless the alliteration ceases immediately.

ROSALINE: I have an idea I think you'll like. (*Takes his hand*) Perhaps we can yet win back our loves.

BUNBURY: Oh, wait! Ernest Jack has dropped his lily. (*Picks it up*)

(*Lights fade as* ROSALINE *drags* BUNBURY *off. Funereal Renaissance music.* ROMEO *speaks in the darkness as lights slowly come up, revealing him bowed over the recumbent* JULIET.)

ROMEO: Eyes look your last!
Arms, take your last embrace! And lips, O you
The doors of breath, seal with a righteous kiss
A dateless bargain to engrossing death!
Come, bitter conduct, come, unsavory guide!
Thou desperate pilot, now at once run on
The dashing rocks thy sea-sick weary bark!

(Lifts a vial to his lips.)
Here's to my love!

BUNBURY: *(Appearing with his lily in some semblance
of Renaissance attire.)* But soft, young master!

ROMEO: Who
Profanes this sacred tomb with pagan life?
Begone—you know not whence these private rites
Arise.

BUNBURY: More than thou canst, brave Romeo,
For I have seen the ending of thy play
And offer thee a feast of love, not worms!

ROMEO: *(Picks up his sword)*
Who art thou, rude trespasser?

BUNBURY: *(Brandishing the lily)* I am he
Who brings the flower of life to bear against
Thy rapier of death. Hath death not claimed
Too many lives this day? Fair Juliet,
And Tybalt, County Paris freshly sent
To pay his fare on Charon's rotten bark?

ROMEO: I am ashamed that all their deaths are mine.

BUNBURY:
This hour the worm has turned. It can be done!
Another flower is saved from cankered bud,
And happiness is yours. Chaste Rosaline!

ROSALINE: *(Appears)*
For I am chaste no more, dear Romeo.
As of this day I am thy only love,
And save thy life so it may live with mine.
Forgive my cold, convented, callous—

BUNBURY: *(Aside, to* ROSALINE*)* Now
Please cease alliteration! It's thy worst,
Most damning fault, you know! For consonants

Are hard and cannot woo a man. But vowels
Will soothe his soul—try assonance instead!

ROSALINE: O Romeo, O glowing bow, though no
More arrows must you throw—

(BUNBURY *is appalled and* ROMEO *looks confused.*
Fortunately, FRIAR LAWRENCE *appears, interrupting*
ROSALINE *making an assonance of herself.*)

FRIAR LAWRENCE:
Alack, alack! What blood is this, which stains
The stony entrance of this sepulcher?
What mean these masterless and gory swords
To lie discolor'd by this place of peace?
(*Sees* ROMEO, ROSALINE *and* BUNBURY.)
Romeo, O, pale! Who else?! 'Tis Rosaline!
What, boy, thy wife is barely dead and you
Defile her tomb with thy adult'rous lust?

JULIET: (*Rising*)
O comfortable friar! Where is my lord?
I do remember well where I should be,
And there I am. Where is my Romeo?

ROMEO: Dear Juliet, you live! The glorious sun
Arising out of darkest night! For thou
Wert dead, but like Our Lord doth live again!
O Easter Day, when sin and fractious feud
Betwixt our families is conquered by
A love that sacrificed itself—

JULIET: My love!
My lord!

ROMEO: My soul! My saint!

BUNBURY: My God!

ROSALINE: (*Trying to intervene*)
I've resurrected both your lives and hope
In gratitude, fair coz, thou shalt give up

Thy claim to me. His life is mine for life,
And in exchange I sacrifice virginity,
Surrendering my cloistered peace to you.

JULIET: Am I to understand you, Rosaline,
That I must render Romeo to thee?

ROSALINE: 'Tis only fair. I've given thee thy life.

JULIET: And in return, thou'lt let me live a nun?
I think not, sister!

BUNBURY: *(Tugging at* ROSALINE*)*
They don't understand!

ROSALINE: From tragedy to brightest joy I've bent
This tale of love betwixt you two. For by
Yourselves you've only blundered near to death!
(Grabbing the poison vial and ROMEO*'s knife.)*
I am the sun! I am the Easter morn!
'Tis I who like Our Lord hath conquered night!

ROMEO: Bright Rosaline, thy wisdom I must not
Deny. Thy clever intervention saved
My life. But thou art not the sun to me.
Thou art the moon, a cooler loveliness.
For warmer beauty stole my heart from thee,
And Juliet, my love, is still my wife.

*(*ROMEO *kisses* JULIET*.)*

ROSALINE: *(Raising the knife, advancing on* JULIET*)*
The life I saved then shall be rendered back!

BUNBURY: *(Grabbing her, wresting the knife away)*
What's done, 'tis done! We must away at once!

ROSALINE: He's mine!

BUNBURY: You've lost him twice! It was not meant
To be!

FRIAR LAWRENCE: Thou brash virago!

ROSALINE: *(Struggling with* BUNBURY*)* Destiny!

(BUNBURY *manages to pull* ROSALINE *out of view.* ROMEO *and* JULIET *keep kissing.*)

FRIAR LAWRENCE:
A leaping glee this morning with it brings.
The sun, in laughter, shines the brighter still.
Go hence to have more talk of these new joys
As Montague and Capulet embrace.
No story could a greater grace bestow
Than this of Juliet and her Romeo.

(*Lights out on the tomb and up on* BUNBURY *alone, holding both the lily and the dagger and still wearing his unusual Renaissance costume.*)

BUNBURY: What a frightfully determined young lady! She had her chance at literary heroism and very nearly committed murder. All for love, of course, so I suppose one must forgive. It seems any crime these days is forgiven if done for love! Imagine if I'd let her stab them? The play would indeed have retained its tragic tone, but if it's been criticized for trafficking in coincidence, what would Oxford dons say of this *deus ex machina* murderess swooping into the tomb and poking the lovers full of holes? So unnecessary, even random, and far too much like life. I'm not at all certain we've improved the play, but I feel so much better, and isn't that what art is all about? Changed it, we have, without a doubt! I'm positively exultant! Just wait till Algy hears this! Cecily *who*?

(*Lighting change reveals several people facing upstage, away from* BUNBURY, *as if playing to an audience located there:* ALGERNON, CECILY, GWENDOLEN, *and* JACK. *Enter* LADY BRACKNELL.)

LADY BRACKNELL: I have missed the last train! My nephew, you seem to be displaying signs of triviality.

JACK: On the contrary, Aunt Augusta, I've now realized—

BUNBURY: Algernon!

(Everyone else freezes for a moment, then turns to see who has spoken.)

LADY BRACKNELL: *(Glaring at* ALGERNON*)* Pray explain who is this neurasthenic young man.

BUNBURY: Neurasthenic? I don't even know what that means!

LADY BRACKNELL: Neither do I, but it describes you perfectly.

BUNBURY: Algy, Rosaline changed the ending!

ALGERNON: The ending of what? We have just arrived at a happy ending here. What a dreadful interruption.

BUNBURY: The ending of *The Tragedy of Romeo and Juliet.*

CECILY: Surely you mean *The Romance of Romeo and Juliet.*

GWENDOLEN: It is my favorite—if scandalous—work of Shakespeare. Why in the world would the ending need changing? It is quite perfect as it is.

LADY BRACKNELL: Indeed it is scandalous, Gwendolen, and I recall expressly forbidding you to read it. No doubt it is the perilous example of young people choosing their own husbands and wives that inspired your adventures in defying parental authority.

BUNBURY: What is the ending?

JACK: Ridiculous fellow! Everyone knows that.

BUNBURY: Do shut up, Jack! Or is it *Ernest*?

ALGERNON: It is Ernest. He's just now changed it back.

BUNBURY: Do Romeo and Juliet die or live?

EVERYONE: Die?

GWENDOLEN: They live, of course! What a ghastly thought! If they had died, half the marriages in the world would fail!

BUNBURY: He never drinks the poison? She never stabs herself?

GWENDOLEN: Certainly not! That ferocious Rosaline bursts in with her mysterious friend and very nearly kills them, then disappears. It makes almost no sense, and is hailed as the first play of the modern era.

JACK: Highly influential on all subsequent literature.

LADY BRACKNELL: To powerful ill effect!

BUNBURY: How absolutely marvelous! I do believe a miracle has occurred!

LADY BRACKNELL: I should hope not. Nothing is more disruptive to nature, not to mention society.

CECILY: My own dear Algernon, who is this peculiarly attractive young man? He seems to be a friend of yours, or at the very least, a vociferous acquaintance.

BUNBURY: *(With great dignity)* I am Bunbury.

JACK: Bunbury is a fiction!

LADY BRACKNELL: A fiction?

BUNBURY: I'm as real as you are!

LADY BRACKNELL: Algernon, you have given us to understand that your friend Bunbury was exploded.

BUNBURY: I am not exploded!

LADY BRACKNELL: On the sound advice of his doctors.

BUNBURY: *(Waving the dagger)* Algy, you know me perfectly well! I'm the least combustible person in Shropshire.

JACK: Look sharp! He's got a dagger!

(CECILY *and* GWENDOLEN *scream.*)

LADY BRACKNELL: Gwendolen, behind me!
I am impenetrable!

(BUNBURY *hides the dagger in his coat.*)

ALGERNON: What utter nonsense! There is a Bunbury,
or was, but this is not he. (*Grabbing* BUNBURY *and
dragging him off.*) Sir, you are interrupting a touching
moment of familial celebration. Be kind enough to
brandish your weaponry elsewhere.

(*They disappear.*)

LADY BRACKNELL: Ernest, I presume this sort of
excitement is not typical in the country. A young girl
conscientiously raised in the city, such as Gwendolen,
is not used to the sudden appearance of incoherent
interlopers from the Renaissance.

JACK: Certainly not, Aunt Augusta. There shall be no
excitement in our marriage whatsoever.

LADY BRACKNELL: I am glad to hear it. Stimulation of
any kind is the dubious privilege of the servant classes.
And now, a carriage, if you please. Lord Bracknell is
not expecting me until the morrow, so I must return
tonight.

(*Lights out on* LADY BRACKNELL, CECILY, GWENDOLEN,
and JACK, *and up on* ALGERNON *and* BUNBURY *alone.*)

ALGERNON: Are you absolutely mad? Not only have
you followed me against my clearly stated wishes,
but have also had the affrontery to—

BUNBURY: To *exist*! How unimaginably horrible!

ALGERNON: We have been perfectly happy with our
arrangement—

BUNBURY: You have been perfectly happy. I have been
perfectly miserable. I languish in Shropshire while you

dash off to the eternal deathbed of that smug and thriving Ernest fellow, who by the way was as rude as could be to me in the copse this morning. He also told me the definition of Bunburying. You have made me a verb!

ALGERNON: Technically, a gerund, I believe.

BUNBURY: In any case, your devotion to Ernest would seem to parallel in many ways your relations with Bunbury, which gives one pause. Not merely a pause, a lacuna! For I don't recall you ever expressing a wish to rechristen yourself after me. Whereas this afternoon you were on your way to the rectory to actually *become* Ernest. What am I to make of that?

ALGERNON: For heaven's sake, Bunbury, I've just found out he is my brother.

BUNBURY: That is disgusting! You are an incestor!

ALGERNON: I am not!

BUNBURY: But you cannot deny you are an invert.

ALGERNON: No worse than you. You are a fiction! And an invert. A fictional invert!

BUNBURY: On the contrary, I am an inverted fiction! And I am deeply sympathetic toward the thwarted Rosaline. I am equally unhappy!

ALGERNON: My dear Bunbury, that is life. Not everyone can be as happy as Madame Bovary!

BUNBURY: I beg your pardon?

ALGERNON: You know that expression. It is practically a cliché. I'm almost ashamed I spoke it.

BUNBURY: As happy as Madame Bovary?

ALGERNON: Yes...surely you've read the novel by Flaubert?

BUNBURY: She's the unhappiest woman in the world!

ALGERNON: Until the end, when she confesses all to her husband and he forgives her.

BUNBURY: That's not what happens. She takes arsenic.

ALGERNON: Apparently Flaubert considered that ending, but, taking the example of Shakespeare, decided instead to make the power of forgiveness his theme.

BUNBURY: Shakespeare?

ALGERNON: Your beloved *Romeo and Juliet. The Romance,* I mean. All anyone need do is explain things properly and it all works out in the end.

BUNBURY: Good heavens! We've changed the lineage of literature!

ALGERNON: We've done no such thing. Bunbury, I fear you've at last gone completely mad. You've certainly driven me mad. Perhaps someday I shall regret this, but—

BUNBURY: Algy, what are you saying?

ALGERNON: You are delightful company, and, as Cecily has noted, peculiarly attractive. You have a slim, gilt soul. I shall always treasure our friendship—

BUNBURY: Our...*friendship*?

ALGERNON: But now that I am about to be married, I realize you are a delightful and peculiar inconvenience.

BUNBURY: An inconvenience!

ALGERNON: I shan't be visiting you in Shropshire any more. When a man starts a family, he must be serious.

BUNBURY: Algy, no!

ALGERNON: You have only your trivial nature to blame.

BUNBURY: I'm absolutely serious. Practically solemn!
You mustn't go.

ALGERNON: I must, I shall, and I am. Farewell.

(ALGERNON *starts to leave, comes back and kisses*
BUNBURY, *looks as if he is about to say something further,*
then rushes out.)

BUNBURY: I should have let her kill them. The world
would be a colder place, but Algy would still be
keeping me warm.

ROSALINE: (*Appearing*) Thou see'st what thou hast
wrought!

BUNBURY: Please, no. I'm too overwrought to round
out your meter. You'll have to take care of your
enjambment yourself.

ROSALINE: Precisely what I've come to tell thee now.
My fate is mine to choose, for 'twas a loose
And dangling thread attendant at the end
Of *Romeo and Juliet.* But I
Embroider truth, and know my way around
(*Takes out the poison vial*)
A loom. I'll trim the selvage edge and hem
The tapestry of literature aright.
(*Starts to drink the poison*)

BUNBURY: That's quite enough of that! (*Wresting the*
poison from her) I can't let you poison yourself, however
much you deserve it for hyperextending that metaphor!

ROSALINE: The thought of losing Romeo is foul
Enough—'twere greater comfort were he dead!
He lives in Juliet's embrace, so I
Now only seek th'embrace of death!
Thou thwartst me once again—thy greatest skill!

BUNBURY: I just hate seeing people die. It's so
unnecessary and indecorous, especially in the young.

ROSALINE: Thou hast a heart of mallow.

BUNBURY: I can't help it. I fear we've altered all of literature, made it frightfully optimistic with our happy ending of *Romeo and Juliet.*

ROSALINE: 'Twas not happy for me.

BUNBURY: And possibly not happy for literature. Algernon only knows *Madame Bovary* in a bowdlerized version that sounds like an utter travesty. Where is pity? Where is terror?

ROSALINE: *(Hopeful)* Might we then change it back?

BUNBURY: Come with me! If we've done some violence to the canon with— *(Holds up the lily)* —This, then we should inspect the damage and consider mitigations. Romeo and Algy could yet be ours!

ROSALINE: Then may we yet find love amid the ruins?

BUNBURY: It seems that is the only place to look!

(They rush off. Music and lighting change. A nineteenth-century LAWYER *sits thinking at his desk, looking remarkably like Edgar Allen Poe. The lighting change reveals a bust of Pallas.)*

LAWYER: Once upon a midnight dreary, while I
   pondered, weak and weary
Over many a quaint and curious volume of forgotten
   lore—
While I nodded, nearly napping, suddenly there came a
   tapping
(Tapping sound)
As of someone gently rapping, rapping at my chamber
   door.
"Tis some visitor," I muttered, "tapping at my chamber
   door—
Only this and nothing more." Presently my soul grew
   stronger; hesitating then no longer

"Sir," said I, "or Madam, truly your forgiveness I
    implore:
But the fact is I was napping, and so gently you came
    rapping
And so faintly you came tapping, tapping at my
    chamber door,
That I scarce was sure I heard you" —here I opened
    wide the door—
(Flings open the door)
Darkness there, and nothing more.
Open then—
(Opens window)

—I flung the shutter, when, with many a flirt and flutter
In there stepped a stately Peacock of the saintly days of
    yore
(A PEACOCK [puppet or projection] comes in and sits on the
bust of Pallas.)
Not the least obeisance made he; not a minute stopped
    or stayed he,
But with mien of lord or lady, perched above my
    chamber door—
Perched, and sat, and nothing more.

Then the rainbow bird beguiling my sad fancy into
    smiling,
By the grave and stern decorum of the countenance it
    wore
"Thou art large and not a wee cock, wouldst," I said,
    "thou like some tea, cock?
Brightly clad and sparkling Peacock wandering on the
    midnight chime
Tell me what thy lordly name is in the Night's
Plutonian prime
Quoth the Peacock—

PEACOCK: (Cheerfully) Anytime!

(The LAWYER's *grim mood is instantly brightened and he breaks into a broad grin.)*

LAWYER: Quoth the Peacock—

PEACOCK: *(Spreading its tail feathers proudly and happily)* Anytime!

(Lights out on the LAWYER *and* PEACOCK, *and up on a Russian drawing room, circa 1900. It is midday—there is cheerful sunshine outside.* OLGA, *wearing the regulation dark-blue dress of a secondary school mistress, is correcting her pupils' work, standing or walking about as she does so.* MASHA, *in a black dress, is sitting reading a book, her hat on her lap.* IRENA, *in white, stands lost in thought.)*

OLGA: It's a year to the day that Father died. The fifth of May—your saint's day, Irena. It was freezing, and snowing very hard. I remember thinking I'd never make it, never survive his death. You'd fainted, and were lying there like you were dead, too. A year later, and we can talk about it without tears—it's almost easy. You're in white, your face is simply glowing—

(A clock strikes twelve.)

OLGA: Noon. I have a memory of that clock striking, too. *(Pause)* Remember the military band that escorted Father to the grave? The guns fired in salute because he was a general? Too bad so few people came. But it was raining pretty hard, sleeting, even snowing.

IRENA: Must we dwell on such sad memories?

MASHA: *(Slamming her book closed, with great decision)* Who wants to go to Moscow?

IRENA: I do!

OLGA: I do!

MASHA: Then let's go right now!

(They all rush out, giggling. Lighting change reveals Bunbury *isolated in light, still holding his lily.)*

BUNBURY: How positively extraordinary! Cheerful endings everywhere! Some works of literature cut so short they barely exist—so full of sorrow and indecision they must have been before Romeo found happiness with Juliet. The Ancient Mariner chooses not to kill the albatross! Bartleby the Scrivener finally prefers to do something! *The Sorrows of Young Werther* retitled *The Pleasant Youth of Grinning Werther!*

ROSALINE: *(Dashing in, out of breath)* It's the same everywhere!

BUNBURY: What have you seen?

ROSALINE: Faust refused the Devil's bargain and went on to become a monk. Miss Havisham got married and had a dozen children. And Candide decided to plant a garden *at the beginning* of the book!

BUNBURY: All of this because you—the mysterious and unseen Rosaline—actually put in an appearance in *Romeo and Juliet*!

ROSALINE: Don't blame it all on me! You were there too, with your ridiculous lily, preventing me from killing them.

BUNBURY: I blame no one. I've decided it's wonderful. You have tremendous power.

ROSALINE: It's a terrible power. And I'm not at all certain I've used it wisely. With all these characters so damn happy, does literature retain its relevance?

BUNBURY: Surely it must. Literature forms the minds of everyone to some degree.

ROSALINE: But it can't change the world without reflecting real conflict and pain. You mentioned pity and terror—Aristotle must be rolling in his grave!

BUNBURY: I very much doubt it. I'm rather certain he was cremated.

ROSALINE: All this from one small change!

BUNBURY: I wonder what more we could change.

ROSALINE: More! Haven't we done enough?

BUNBURY: What other unseen characters share your power? The power of the unexpected! Imagine if they all joined forces! Perhaps we could indeed change the world! Would Algy think me trivial then?

ROSALINE: Just like any man! Always out to change the world. Can't you just be satisfied with not making it any worse?

BUNBURY: Come with me!

ROSALINE: No!

BUNBURY: I came with you!

ROSALINE: And you see the result! You're assaulting five thousand years of culture!

BUNBURY: Five thousand years of suffering! If we can eliminate pity and terror from literature, perhaps we can eliminate it from life! Bring peace to the world!

ROSALINE: This is a personal vendetta.

BUNBURY: Whatever do you mean?

ROSALINE: To prove yourself more than a trivial little Bunbury, you'd jeopardize the history of the world. All to impress your tedious Algernon.

BUNBURY: This isn't about Algy! I'll show you it's not! You've no idea what you're talking about.

ROSALINE: You're obsessed with significance.

BUNBURY: Well...wouldn't you like to *matter*?

ROSALINE: Bunbury, that's sweet—in a naïve and demented sort of way, but you see what disasters result from changing literature of the past.

BUNBURY: Then come with me to the future!

(BUNBURY *takes* ROSALINE's *hand.*)

ROSALINE: Next you'll offer me the chance to become a real live girl!

(BUNBURY *pulls* ROSALINE *off as the lights change, coming up on small-town Southern park in moonlight. Perhaps a fountain or statue of an angel. Summer insect noises. ALLAN, a poetic youth dressed in clean, tasteful early Depression-era clothing, tries to look nonchalant, but he's obviously quite keyed up.* BUNBURY, *now in clothes similar to* ALLAN's, *shows up, smoking a cigarette. He still has his lily.*)

BUNBURY: (*Seductively, and with great confidence.*) I have dreams in my pocket.

ALLAN: (*Nervously, with a charming Southern accent*) I beg your pardon?

BUNBURY: I have tricks up my sleeve.

ALLAN: Nice lily.

BUNBURY: Thanks.

ALLAN: I fail to recognize you, sir. And your accent— is it English?

BUNBURY: Indeed. Cigarette?

ALLAN: Oh, no! I mean, I don't—

(BUNBURY *proffers the cigarette.*)

ALLAN: Sure.

BUNBURY: *(Lighting the cigarette off his own, sexy)*
A cigarette is a perfect type of a perfect pleasure.
It is exquisite—

ALLAN: And it leaves one unsatisfied. *(Takes a drag, coughs)*

BUNBURY: Extraordinary! That's exactly what I was about to say.

ALLAN: You wouldn't be the first.

BUNBURY: Nothing is original. Everything is a quote, even when one is not conscious of the fact.

ALLAN: Mister Oscar Wilde.

BUNBURY: Who is he?

ALLAN: *Was* he. You're joking, surely?

BUNBURY: Never heard of him. Irish?

ALLAN: He was—a very famous—author—
from before the War.

BUNBURY: What war?

ALLAN: The Great War!

BUNBURY: A *great* war! How dreadful! Did this Mister Wilde write about the war?

ALLAN: No, he was known for— *(Hesitates)*

BUNBURY: Known for what?

ALLAN: He had some troubles of a personal nature. *(Embarrassed)* How long is your visit to Laurel?

BUNBURY: I will sojourn here only briefly. I am on a world tour.

ALLAN: That's awfully exciting.

BUNBURY: *(Gesturing toward* ALLAN's *hand)* I see you are married.

ALLAN: *(Nervously touching his ring)* Only just.
I'm not used to this yet. It's chafing a bit.

BUNBURY: Perhaps you need a larger size.

ALLAN: Could be. *(Pause)* My wife is out of town.
A family illness.

BUNBURY: And you miss her.

ALLAN: It's difficult to say. We have a mutual love of
poetry, can't stop talking about it. Browning, Dickinson,
even Swinburne. And Oscar Wilde—he was a poet, too.
We always have such interesting things to say to one
another.

BUNBURY: But.

ALLAN: I miss that part of her. Someone to talk to.
I don't suppose you like poetry?

BUNBURY: I adore it.

ALLAN: But you don't know Oscar Wilde. Everyone
who adores poetry knows Oscar Wilde.

BUNBURY: I'm naturally drawn to literature of a certain
type. Did he write of star-crossed love?

ALLAN: In a manner of speaking...

BUNBURY: Like beautiful bodies of the dead who had
  not grown old
And they shut them, with tears, in a magnificent
  mausoleum,
With roses at the head and jasmine at the feet—
That is how desires look that have passed
Without fulfillment, without one of them having
  achieved
A night of sensual delight, or a moonlit morn.

ALLAN: That's Cavafy!

BUNBURY: An early poem called *Desires*. But Cavafy is
terribly modern. So you see, I am well versed.

ALLAN: Do you read Greek?

BUNBURY: Perfectly.

ALLAN: My wife says she doesn't like Cavafy. But secretly she does. I have a volume of his poetry at home, but I have to hide it. I can't read the Greek part, and I'm sure the translation doesn't do him justice.

BUNBURY: I could read the Greek for you.

ALLAN: Oh! Could you? But...it's late.

BUNBURY: Is your home nearby?

ALLAN: Yes, but—

BUNBURY: You were just out for a walk before bedtime.

ALLAN: Yes. To settle the nerves. I'm the nervous sort.

BUNBURY: A walk and a cigarette.

ALLAN: Except that I don't smoke. *(Laughs)* This is my first time!

BUNBURY: Is it?

ALLAN: Yes. *(Pause)* The moon seems especially bright tonight. You can see all the features, craters and such. And the Sea of Tranquility. You could almost go wading in it! *(Pause)* I would like to learn a little Greek.

BUNBURY: It can be done.

(They smoke. Lights out on them and up on BLANCHE *sitting in a train compartment reading, fashionably dressed for 1930. Train sounds. After a moment,* ROSALINE *appears, now in Depression-era American clothes.)*

ROSALINE: Pardon me. Is this seat taken?

BLANCHE: Oh, no. Certainly not! Please join me. I was enjoying a slim volume of poetry, but it is—as you can see—very slim, and I was on the verge of exhausting its charms.

ROSALINE: *(Sitting down)* Thank you so much.

BLANCHE: What a lovely English accent you have!

ROSALINE: It is Italian.

BLANCHE: Oh! I've been to neither Italy nor England, so I suppose I have confused the two. But I have traveled the world— *(Holds up the book)* —Through literature!

ROSALINE: Beware of literature.

BLANCHE: Oh, I know. It can be so—*seductive,* can't it? My husband and I were drawn together by literature, by poetry! We read aloud quite often, alternating stanzas. We've almost finished *The Faerie Queene.*

ROSALINE: I'm sorry. We haven't time for fairy queens.

BLANCHE: I beg your pardon? We have half an hour at least before the next stop, my stop—

ROSALINE: You will soon be—tempted—to change your life. To be persuaded—I'm sorry—I have no idea how to tell you this!

BLANCHE: To tell me what? You are a positive soothsayer, whoever you are! Who are you?

ROSALINE: You may call me Rosaline.

BLANCHE: Rosaline! Straight out of Shakespeare!

ROSALINE: Exactly. But if you care about literature, you must listen to me. Whatever happens, you must act naturally. Don't deviate from your path.

BLANCHE: My path! You are a charming train compartment companion, Miss Rosaline, but whatever would you know about my path? You don't even know my name.

ROSALINE: Your name is Blanche, is it not? And you are going to Laurel, Mississippi?

BLANCHE: Oh, now, who put you up to this?
Was it Allan?

ROSALINE: No, not your husband. He doesn't even
know I exist. I have so much to tell you, and you
must listen carefully.

BLANCHE: *(Unnerved, she takes out a flask.)* Very well.
But I must have a little drink—just a tiny nip, and
only one—to steady my nerves! *(Looks out the window)*
Oh, look at that moon! Doesn't it seem too large this
evening? Almost menacing?

*(BLANCHE takes a big drink while ROSALINE watches her
nervously and the lights fade on the two of them. At the
same time, the lights come up on a bedroom. BUNBURY and
ALLAN are in the bed, naked, with moonlight shining on
them through the window.)*

ALLAN: That was *lots* better than a poem! May I have
another cigarette?

BUNBURY: *(Lighting cigarettes for both of them)* Certainly,
young man.

ALLAN: Please don't call me "young man". It's eerie.
You may call me Allan. And your name is...?

BUNBURY: *(Hesitates for a moment, braced for ridicule)*
Bunbury.

ALLAN: Oh, now that is too funny! You don't know
Oscar Wilde, but you quote him without cease!

BUNBURY: It is my name, not an epigram.

ALLAN: It's a character from one of Mister Wilde's
plays—well, not exactly a character, but a concept.
A very amusing one. *(Thinks a moment)* That I never
fully understood until now! *(Notices that BUNBURY is
quite silent)* What's wrong? You're suddenly silent,
and that doesn't seem your nature.

BUNBURY: In what play does the character Bunbury appear?

ALLAN: That's just the thing—he never does!

(BUNBURY *blanches*.)

ALLAN: Algernon pretends he's visiting his sick friend Bunbury in the country—

BUNBURY: —Whenever he needs an excuse to get away from London.

ALLAN: It's a marvelous conceit. Very clever of Mister Wilde. Bunburying, it's called.

BUNBURY: The play?

ALLAN: No, no—the play is called *The Importance of Being Earnest*. It's terribly famous. How can you know Cavafy—who's still relatively obscure in this country— and not know *Earnest*? The scene when Cecily and Gwendolen think they are both engaged to the same Ernest is unbearably comic!

BUNBURY: Cecily and Gwendolen?

ALLAN: (*Rummages on a bookshelf*) Cecily is engaged to Algernon and Gwendolen to Jack, who in the end turns out to be Ernest after all. I'll loan you my copy if you promise to give it back. (*Proffers a copy of the play*)

BUNBURY: (*Grabs the play and pages through it*) Algy and Jack or Ernest—all simply characters...?

ALLAN: Algernon explains Bunburying to Jack right at the beginning.

BUNBURY: (*Finds the passage, gasps*) This is Algy to a T!

ALLAN: I'm of the opinion it's the best play of the nineteenth century, and possibly the twentieth, at least so far.

BUNBURY: And Bunbury never appears?

ALLAN: He only existed in Algernon's mind.

BUNBURY: Dear heaven! I'm a fiction—a fantasy!

ALLAN: Oh, no! I've had fantasies before, and you're as real as I am.

BUNBURY: That's certainly true.

ALLAN: What?

BUNBURY: Never mind. You're too young to understand.

ALLAN: I understand it all, now! (*Jumps on* BUNBURY) Let's do it again!

(BLANCHE, *still in conversation with* ROSALINE, *barges into the room.*)

BLANCHE: I am devoted to fiction, but not when it concerns my own life. Where is that boy—?

(BLANCHE *gasps and freezes when she sees* ALLAN *and* BUNBURY *naked and entangled. They freeze, too.*)

BLANCHE: I thought...this room was empty. But it isn't empty. It has two people in it. My young husband and an older man—

BUNBURY: I beg your pardon! An *older* man?!

ALLAN: He's been my friend for years!

ROSALINE: (*Following* BLANCHE *into the room*) Bunbury, darling, you must give this up!

(BLANCHE *start to leave.* BUNBURY, *wrapped in the sheet, jumps up and stops her.*)

BUNBURY: No, no, Blanche, please don't run off. You mustn't pretend you didn't see! You won't be able to hold it in, and when you explode, Allan will kill himself!

BLANCHE: Let go of me, you horrid creature! Who are you?

ROSALINE: He's just as I described. A misguided soul out to pervert literature.

BLANCHE: You *are* a pervert! You disgust me!

ALLAN: Blanche, Blanche, I'm sorry. It shouldn't have happened this way, but it was bound to eventually. We both always knew it.

BLANCHE: Allan, I am frozen. I am petrified with revulsion. Please don't come near me.

ALLAN: I couldn't bear it if you hated me. I love you so much.

ROSALINE: Reject him. He has destroyed you.

BUNBURY: *(Putting on his clothes)* Rosaline! We can save them. We can save them both.

ROSALINE: *(Pulls out her vial of poison)* Here, young man. You are humiliated and your life is over. Drink this.

ALLAN: BUNBURY:
(Grabbing the vial)   Rosaline, you're being
Is it poison?   perfectly horrible!

ROSALINE: Very special poison.

BUNBURY: Allan, don't listen to her. She's a persuasive but pedantic reactionary, and if you kill yourself something dreadful will happen to Blanche.

BLANCHE: Something dreadful has already happened to Blanche!

ROSALINE: That's Romeo's poison.

BUNBURY: Stop romanticizing it! He doesn't need to kill himself. Allan, now that Blanche knows what we did—

(BLANCHE *gives a little moan.*)

BUNBURY: —Can you tell her you still love her? That's what she needs to know.

ALLAN: Blanche, of course. Of course, I love you. I'll always love you. I just didn't know who I was till now.

BLANCHE: I knew. I always knew.

ALLAN: And you thought you could save me.

BLANCHE: But you've only pulled me into the quicksand with you!

ALLAN: No one else has ever tried to save me, Blanche. Only you.

BUNBURY: Well, certainly I have, but then again, I don't exist.

ALLAN: Don't hate me, Blanche. Please say you still love me, despite it all. *(Lifts the poison vial to his lips)*

BLANCHE: *(After a moment's struggle)* Allan...I love you.

BUNBURY: *(Grabbing the vial from ALLAN)* Give me that! What a lot of trouble this has caused!

ALLAN: *(Embraces BLANCHE)* We need each other. Not in the way we thought, but in a more profound way.

BLANCHE: *(To ROSALINE)* It's all true, isn't it? Everything you said.

BUNBURY: Did she say anything about Polack rapists and madhouses and losing Belle Reve?

BLANCHE: No.

ROSALINE: If that's her path—

BLANCHE: You would have let me go mad—?

BUNBURY: None of that has to happen now.

BLANCHE: So much for sisterhood! Does this mean I'm free?

ALLAN: Free of our marriage?

BLANCHE: Now, Allan, how could we possibly continue? Even loving each other spiritually as we do? You need some flesh and so do I.

ALLAN: Blanche, this is why we get along so well. You're absolutely right. *(To* BUNBURY*)* Where are you going next on your world tour? New Orleans? New York? San Francisco?

BUNBURY: *(Consults a piece of paper)* The campus of a small college in New England.

ALLAN: I want to go to New England, but not yet. I've saved up a little money, and I think I'll go to New York. If...that's all right with you, Blanche.

BLANCHE: *(Wearily)* Go find your flesh. Revel in carnality!

BUNBURY: *(Taking* BLANCHE'*s hands)* Do you understand, Blanche, what I'm trying to do?

ROSALINE: I explained it all to her. Every absurd notion.

BLANCHE: You've saved me somehow, I think. I just need a— *(She pulls out her flask.)*

BUNBURY: *(Grabbing it)* No!

BLANCHE: You don't let anybody drink anything! It's just Southern Comfort.

BUNBURY: Come with me, Blanche. Rosaline, you too. There's no stopping me now! I've discovered the greatest secret in history!

BLANCHE: You're saving...literature?

BUNBURY: And maybe the world. I know it sounds pretentious,

but—

BLANCHE: I like pretentious. And I like you. You've saved me from the madhouse, if I'm not mistaken. Although I might begrudge you that Polack someday.

(As lights fade on BUNBURY, ROSALINE, BLANCHE, *and* ALLAN, *they come up slowly on a tableau of* GEORGE *cradling* MARTHA *in his arms as she cries. They are in the living room of a house on the campus of a small New England college in 1962. It is very late at night, with sunrise imminent.* MARTHA'*s sobs are quite audible. After a moment,* BUNBURY *comes in cautiously, with quills sticking out of the sleeves and front of his shirt. And he still has the lily.)*

BUNBURY: Excuse me. I know this is an inopportune time.

MARTHA: Jesus H Christ! George, who the hell is this—?

GEORGE: *(Overlapping)* Who the hell are you?

MARTHA: *(Overlapping.)* Who the hell is this light-in-the-loafers Limey and what is he doing in our house at this hour? With a lily, for Chrissakes! If you're looking for a drink, you're out of luck.

GEORGE: That's right. Martha's lapped it all up.

MARTHA: You've done your share of lapping, too, Georgie.

BUNBURY: I'm from Western Union, actually.

GEORGE: Western Union?

MARTHA: What happened to Crazy Billy?

BUNBURY: He was sacked. He gave you the wrong telegram.

MARTHA: What?

GEORGE: If you're Western Union, where's your uniform?

MARTHA: Crazy Billy had a uniform, didn't he, George?

BUNBURY: He had a uniform but the wrong telegram.

MARTHA: The wrong...George, what does this mean? Another game?

GEORGE: Nothing, Martha. Good-bye, Mister Chips—

MARTHA: And what's that sticking out of your sleeves?

BUNBURY: *(Calling out the door)* Now, please.

(ROSALINE and BLANCHE come in escorting JIM, who is just about to turn twenty-one. He has blonde eyes and blue hair.)

GEORGE: Who is that?

JIM: You don't even know me, Dad?

GEORGE & MARTHA: Dad?!

JIM: Your own Sonny-Jim.

GEORGE:
Martha, how'd you pull this together?

MARTHA:
Of course, of course—

MARTHA: You have blonde eyes—

JIM: And blue hair.

MARTHA: Just like we've always said.

JIM: Tried to get rid of me, eh, Dad? Off me just to get back at Mom?

GEORGE: You'll have to admit she—

MARTHA: *(Rushing JIM, her arms outstretched)* My baby! My own baby boy!

JIM: *(Stopping her)* No, Mom. No more of that.

MARTHA: No more of what?

JIM: No more grab-ass with the kiddie. The little bugger. Always coming at me. You're gonna stop it.

MARTHA: Stop what? I never—

JIM: You're gonna stop it because I'm leaving.

MARTHA: You just got here!

JIM: What kind of environment is this for a kid? Profanity screamed twenty-four hours a day— here it is almost dawn and you're still boozing it up.

GEORGE: Well, who wouldn't drink in order to endure your mother?

MARTHA: You believe him, George?

JIM: Not just Mom. It takes two to *totentanz*, Dad.

GEORGE:	MARTHA:
Oh, German, very good.	Strindberg! Idiot!

GEORGE: Smart boy!

MARTHA: Takes after me.

JIM: I always knew, Dad, about your novel. The one Grandpa White Mouse wouldn't let you publish and you hid in that smelly wooden box I made in Junior Achievement.

GEORGE: You read it?

JIM: It was in my box. I was supposed to read it, wasn't I? Why didn't you have the—you know—

MARTHA: The guts!

JIM: The guts to publish it? To defy Grandpa White Mouse and see if he dared fire his only son-in-law? He might have admired you for it! For standing up to him. For showing some—

MARTHA & JIM: Guts!

JIM: Who needs a goddam academic job when you've written a novel—based on personal experience— a novel of painful honesty and deep sensitivity? A

novel festered to life over years of torment but not
flinching. Why didn't you publish it, Dad? With the
shape this country's in, the market is panting for it.
Lusting to get their hands on your dirty secrets.
But instead you killed it. Aborted it. Out of a profound
lack of—

MARTHA, JIM, BUNBURY, BLANCHE: Guts!!

(BUNBURY *runs outside.*)

JIM: Just like you tried to kill me tonight. Had it all
figured out so it would look like an accident. On a
moonlit night on a country road with my learner's
permit in my pocket-

MARTHA:	JIM:
I meant to ask, what's he	—I would have swerved
doing with learner's permit	to avoid a porcupine and
at twenty years old?	driven straight into a—

JIM & GEORGE: Large tree! But you (I) didn't.

GEORGE: Why not? No car, no tree—?

(BUNBURY *runs in with a porcupine [puppet] in his arms.*)

BUNBURY: No porcupine! I snatched it out of the way!
(Reacting to the quills) Ow! Ow!

JIM: So of course I stopped, because anybody who
would grab a porcupine from in front of a speeding
car is either incredibly kind-hearted or out of his mind.

ROSALINE: Both, let me assure you.

BUNBURY: Ow!

JIM: And these people have explained it all to me.
I shoulda just kept driving, but this nice fellow
persuaded me I needed to tell you—

BLANCHE: That you're the worst parents in the entire
world, fictional or otherwise. Mister Charles Dickens
at his most depressing couldn't have imagined more

monstrous progenitors! *(To* JIM*)* Young man. Young, young, young man. Have you ever read *The Arabian Nights?*

JIM: It's my favorite!

BLANCHE: *(Taking his hand)* Well, just call me Scheherazade and let's go. I have stories for you. Let me take you away from all this depravity— to a world of fantasy!

JIM: But I'm only twenty.

BLANCHE: Why, that makes you a fantasy in and of yourself!

MARTHA: George, you ninny, don't just let him go!

GEORGE: Martha, you heard what he said. He's disowning us.

MARTHA: Disowning you!

GEORGE: And you!

MARTHA: He just got here, for Chrissakes! Stop him!

GEORGE: Jim!

JIM: *(At the door with* BLANCHE*)* Yes, Dad.

GEORGE: So...you liked it?

JIM: Liked what?

GEORGE: My novel.

JIM: *(After a moment)* Yeah, Dad. It was good. You could still publish it. *(To* BUNBURY*)* Couldn't he?

BUNBURY: It can be done.

*(*JIM *and* BLANCHE *leave.* MARTHA *smacks* GEORGE.*)*

MARTHA: He got away! You let our son get away.

GEORGE: He'll be back. No one could stay with a woman like that very long.

(MARTHA *smacks* GEORGE *again.*)

GEORGE: And he liked it, Martha.

MARTHA: I did, too, George. I did, too.

GEORGE: You read it?

MARTHA: Of course. But I couldn't tell my father.

GEORGE: Why now, Martha? Why tell me now?
(Kisses her tenderly)

MARTHA: You gave me a son, George. A son.

ROSALINE & BUNBURY: *(To each other)* Ibsen?

(Lights out on MARTHA *and* GEORGE, *which isolates*
BUNBURY *and* ROSALINE *in light. The porcupine gives*
a little screech.)

BUNBURY: *(Dropping the porcupine)* Ow!

(The porcupine runs away into the darkness. ROSALINE
starts pulling quills from BUNBURY'*s arms.)*

BUNBURY: Now that wasn't so disastrous, was it?
The boy had his say and the parents seem to have
some kind of future together. What profound work
we are doing! Ow!

ROSALINE: And yet...what has it gotten us, Bunbury?

BUNBURY: My dear Rosaline! It's gotten us all manner
of—why, *look* what it's gotten us—!

ROSALINE: My arms are empty—here's no Romeo,
And neither is your Algernon in sight!

BUNBURY: Stop it this instant! You're reverting to blank
verse and the form is no longer relevant to modern
society.

ROSALINE: You've not become any more relevant,
nor any less trivial.

BUNBURY: We've amended major works of literature! What could be more significant?

ROSALINE: You can't change the world from within the pages of a book. Certainly not these days.

BUNBURY: You may be right. Allan said there's been a Great War.

ROSALINE: Jim told me of a worse one. The world is still a wretched place, despite your quixotic quest.

BUNBURY: All the same, I'm quite hurt you think I'm still trivial.

ROSALINE: I'm sorry, darling, but it's so. You abandon these boys as soon as you've saved them. What could be more trivial than that?

BUNBURY: Like any young man disappointed in love, I've become promiscuous.

ROSALINE: And we've ruint a lot of perfect lovely literature.

BUNBURY: (Sighs) You're right. I'm worse than before. Less than before! Alone!

ROSALINE: I abandoned Romeo to my cousin, just as you've abandoned Algernon.

BUNBURY: I must remind you, they abandoned us first.

ROSALINE: I don't suppose we are *entirely* alone.

BUNBURY: We have each other, fictional though we are.

ROSALINE: Mired in mutual misfortune.

BUNBURY: And complicit in its complication. Oh dear, we're alliterating again.

ROSALINE: Might something yet be done?

BUNBURY: After four hundred years in your case and sixty-five in mine?

ROSALINE: I have a thought. Give me my poison and the dagger.

BUNBURY: Whatever for?

ROSALINE: Come with me to Verona.

BUNBURY: *(Takes out the poison vial and the dagger)* For whom do you intend these?

ROSALINE: 'Tis Juliet stands in my way.

BUNBURY: You mustn't!

ROSALINE: *(Snatches the vial and dagger)* I shall, and you'll help—darling!

BUNBURY: We can't go backwards.

ROSALINE: Yes, we can. Sometimes it's the only way to go. *(Grabbing his hand)*

(Unseen by BUNBURY and ROSALINE, ROMEO appears, then hides as a very pregnant JULIET waddles by, a shade and a half of her former self. JULIET does not see ROMEO and she leaves.)

BUNBURY: Oh, dear, it's almost certain to be depressing.

ROSALINE: Happy endings often are.

(Lighting change puts them in the same space as ROMEO as he reappears from hiding.)

ROMEO: My Rosaline! Why art thou dressed so strange?

ROSALINE: My order's habit changed.

ROMEO: Yes, quite a bit!
And lily-man as well. Good-day, sirrah!

BUNBURY: Sirrah, I am!? Then I'll away. Farewell!
(Leaves)

ROSALINE: No, Bunbury, I need you here with me!

ROMEO: 'Tis well enough he's gone. I've sought thee out
For countless days—

ROSALINE: They seem like centuries!

ROMEO: Thy cousin Juliet is great with child.

ROSALINE: Congratulations to you both, I'm sure.

ROMEO: 'Twill be our eighth.

ROSALINE: The eighth?!

ROMEO: The thrill is gone.
My lust is quenched. I've sired a clam'ring brood
I can't afford to feed. But 'tis my fate
And can't be altered save by God in heav'n.

ROSALINE: Perhaps it could yet change.

ROMEO: What meanest thou?

ROSALINE:
Thy fate was skewed within my family's tomb
When Juliet awakened to thy face.
But come with me, and fate may prove a bawd,
Accommodating ardor for a fee.

(*Lighting change reveals the Capulet tomb with* JULIET *lying as she did before [not pregnant].*)

ROMEO: (*Not yet seeing* JULIET)
Thy order's habit's changed in many ways—

ROSALINE: Pray listen close. Confusing this will seem
At first, but let me shepherd thee and all
Will be as clear and bright as sun's first glow.

ROMEO: Thou art a dazzling sun unto mine eye!

ROSALINE: When once I was the wise but chilly moon!
Refrain from praise a moment, sir. I must
Instruct you on the way to change your fate.
When Juliet awakes, tell her thy heart
Has fickle grown again, and thou art mine—

ROMEO: (*Grabbing her sensually, perhaps roughly*)
And mine thou art as well, she needn't know—

ROSALINE: 'Tis well she might, as I will be thy wife!

ROMEO:
Thou murderest romance with words like "wife".
If words you want, try "concubine" instead.

ROSALINE: What concubine?

ROMEO: If I am married, thou
My mistress be!

ROSALINE: Thy manly shape doth shrink
Before mine eye. Thy noble vows shrug off
And double wives thou wantst in bigamy?
I've learnt a thing or two from literature!
Art not the man I loved and thought loved me!
(Handing him the dagger)
Take back thy dagger and with it, my curse!
(Turns her back on him and takes out the poison vial)
'Twere best I never lived to see this day!

ROMEO: In youth I thought that love between a man
And wife was holiest and best.

*(ROSALINE, in despair, drinks but does not yet swallow,
listening.)*

ROMEO: But now
I've learned that love cannot survive the shocks
Of childbirth, daily life, and countless years
Of seeing just one slowly aging face
Upon the pillow next to mine. Instead
A hundred faces have I seen, well, not
Exactly seen—'twas sometimes dark! But fall
In love I have a thousand times since thee,
And yet I want to kiss thee as if first!
*(With a full mouth and a terrible look in her eye,
she turns toward him.)*
Aye, chaste and winsome Rosaline, now meet
The love thy order bidst thee never greet!

(They kiss passionately and deeply. After a moment, he chokes and staggers back.)

ROMEO: *(Gasping)*
Thy pungent kiss is not done by the book!

ROSALINE: *(Spits)*
But have thy lips the sin that they have took!

(ROMEO dies, falling back into the tomb, near JULIET.)

ROSALINE: *(Spits)*
Thy bitter poison is returned to thee
So thou might rest in chaste nobility!

(ROSALINE quickly retires to the shadows to watch as FRIAR LAWRENCE enters as before.)

FRIAR LAWRENCE:
Alack, alack! What blood is this, which stains
The stony entrance of this sepulcher?

(ROSALINE spits. FRIAR LAWRENCE hears, looks puzzled.)

FRIAR LAWRENCE:
What mean these masterless and gory swords
To lie discolor'd by this place of peace?
Romeo, O, pale! What, Paris, too?
And steep'd in blood? Ah, what an unkind hour
Is guilty of this lamentable chance!
The lady stirs.

JULIET: *(Rising)*
O comfortable friar! Where is my lord?
I do remember well where I should be,
And there I am. Where is my Romeo?

(JULIET shrieks when she sees ROMEO dead, and falls upon his corpse. Lights fade on the tomb and come up on ROSALINE and BUNBURY.)

BUNBURY: *(Aghast)* Thou art a murderess!

ROSALINE: How could I kill
A man who planned to kill himself e'en so?
'Twas his own poison given back, and his
Own words that brought about his death this time.

BUNBURY: You've undone all we've done!

ROSALINE: Not all, but most.
I sacrifice my happiness for sake
Of literature. 'Tis more artistic and
More poignant with this end.

BUNBURY: You could not have
Him on your terms and therefore chose his death!

ROSALINE: And mine as well. I have erased myself
From Shakespeare's greatest play. I'm but a thought,
A mere ideal, never seen upon
The stage. I much prefer myself this way!
Our meddling in the lives of fictions hath
Not changed the world at all. We are, in fact,
More trivial for our insistence on
A role.

BUNBURY: I would erase myself as well
If I believed I meant so little to
The world. If Algernon was right to leave,
Not love—

ROSALINE: Then show to me a work of art
That changed by thee can truly change this earth.

BUNBURY: Then so I shall! And to myself give birth!

(Lights out on BUNBURY *and up on a country road and a tree. Two sorry-looking tramps,* VLADIMIR *and* ESTRAGON *stand before the tree, staring up at it. After a moment,* BUNBURY *appears with his lily.)*

VLADIMIR: Gogo, who's that?

ESTRAGON: Didi, could it be—?

VLADIMIR: *(Astonished and delighted.)* Godot!

ESTRAGON: You've come at last!

(Lights out on them and up on OLD ALGERNON *reading in his study. He is quite elderly. The study, sparsely furnished, is clearly not Victorian, and includes, among other modern conveniences, a television.* OLD CECILY *appears, looking frighteningly like* LADY BRACKNELL.)

OLD CECILY: Algernon!

OLD ALGERNON: *(Barely looking up from his book)* Yes, my dear.

OLD CECILY: It is very nearly time!

OLD ALGERNON: Already?

OLD CECILY: Really, Algernon, it is almost disgraceful what little regard you have for the modern world. Lost in your books, you've ignored, missed, or simply forgotten every significant event of the last seventy-five years.

OLD ALGERNON: Cecily, my dear, in the long run— I mean the truly long run that encompasses the formation of our solar system and the birth and death of galaxies—in the long run, what events of the last seventy-five years have any lasting significance?

OLD CECILY: Significance is subjective, as anyone knows. Last week's cricket results won't send a planet careening off its axis, but to a small boy in Eastcheap, they are everything.

OLD ALGERNON: And to me, my work is everything.

OLD CECILY: I am painfully aware of the fact. I only remind you in case you wish to witness an event of significance to everyone on this particular planet.

OLD ALGERNON: To everyone, or just Americans, my dear?

OLD CECILY: To everyone, Algernon. I shall be watching downstairs, should you wish to join me.

OLD ALGERNON: Perhaps, dear. Perhaps.

(OLD CECILY leaves. After a moment, HARTLEY appears, not looking a day older than he did when working for BUNBURY.)

HARTLEY: A gentleman to see you, sir.

OLD ALGERNON: Really? I didn't hear the door.

HARTLEY: He did not use the door, sir. I discovered him in the library.

(BUNBURY comes in without his lily, not a minute older than when he first appeared.)

BUNBURY: Algy.

OLD ALGERNON: Good heavens! Bunbury! Where the devil have you been for the last seventy-odd years?

BUNBURY: I might ask you the same.

OLD ALGERNON: My academic career is a matter of public record. Your disappearance, however, is a mystery to all concerned.

BUNBURY: All concerned? And what tiny subset of the world population finds my whereabouts of any significance?

OLD ALGERNON: Myself, Bunbury. I have concerned myself with your whereabouts.

BUNBURY: For the last seventy-something years?

OLD ALGERNON: You are looking remarkably well.

BUNBURY: And you are looking...

OLD ALGERNON: I am looking ninety-six years old. You, however, don't look a day over twenty-two.

BUNBURY: I've a picture in my attic.

OLD ALGERNON: I beg your pardon?

BUNBURY: Literary joke. Obscure author. Never mind.

OLD ALGERNON: I am rather an expert on all authors, especially of the last seventy-five years.

BUNBURY: Not this one, believe me. Your life seems quite comfortable. I see you have engaged Hartley.

OLD ALGERNON: Who?

BUNBURY: Your butler. He used to work for me.

OLD ALGERNON: I hadn't noticed. Perhaps you'll think me a dreadful pedant, but I must insist you tell me the name of that author. Otherwise I shall go mad.

BUNBURY: You could very well go mad if I tell you.

(OLD ALGERNON *looks expectant.*)

BUNBURY: Oscar Wilde.

OLD ALGERNON: Who?

BUNBURY: His name is Oscar Wilde.

OLD ALGERNON: Never heard of him.

BUNBURY: I only became aware of him by accident myself, but apparently he wrote several important plays, numerous essays, children's stories, and one decadent novella.

OLD ALGERNON: English?

BUNBURY: Irish.

OLD ALGERNON: Well, then!

BUNBURY: You are unaware of him, Algy, because he is *your* author. Or rather *our* author, as we are both characters in his play *The Importance of Being Earnest.*

OLD ALGERNON: Good heavens! What nonsense!

BUNBURY: It's true, Algy. You always accused me of triviality, when in fact you yourself are a work of fiction!

OLD ALGERNON: I've lived a long and productive non-fictional life!

BUNBURY: How do you know it is non-fictional?

OLD ALGERNON: Because it has been so damned boring! No author would write such tedium.

BUNBURY: I suspect he did not. But once created, once imagined by the author and all his readers, you had a life beyond the play, into your career, your marriage— you did marry Cecily, did you not?

OLD ALGERNON: *(With some regret)* Oh, yes.

BUNBURY: Your financially secure life has been imagined by countless people, from cocksure youth to fragile age.

OLD ALGERNON: But what of you? If we're both characters, shouldn't you be ninety-six as well?

BUNBURY: Apparently I never appear the actual play. I am a plot device, a mere joke, and no one—including the author—ever imagined me having a life at all. Therefore, I've never aged. I'm a sort of literary vampire, I suppose.

OLD ALGERNON: Then how do you exist at all? Someone must have imagined you.

BUNBURY: You did. I'm rather certain you gave me life. *(Produces* ALLAN's *copy of* The Importance of Being Ernest*)* Here's the play.

*(*BUNBURY *points out a passage.* OLD ALGERNON *reads it for a moment.)*

OLD ALGERNON: Why on earth have you waited this long to tell me?

BUNBURY: It took me seventy-odd years to work it out. If I'd known, I would have just changed this— *(Indicates book)* —And saved myself rather a lot of trouble.

OLD ALGERNON: You've spent all this time trying to prove to me—?

BUNBURY: Nobody is trivial. Even someone fictional can change everything.

OLD ALGERNON: And now? *(Thumbing to the end of the play)* Are we still in the play? Or the real world?

BUNBURY: I'm not at all convinced there is a real world.

OLD ALGERNON: That sounds suspiciously like modern literary theory. Possibly even French.

BUNBURY: Which you clearly disdain.

OLD ALGERNON: As Cecily often reminds me, my own research is quite irrelevant to the modern world.

BUNBURY: What is your academic speciality?

OLD ALGERNON: The lily motif.

BUNBURY: The lily motif? That sound rather more like art history!

OLD ALGERNON: You don't know the lily motif?

BUNBURY: No.

OLD ALGERNON: The mysterious Man with a Lily who appears—or is referenced—in several of the most significant works of literature since 1947.

BUNBURY: *A Streetcar Named Desire?*

OLD ALGERNON: It is the Man with the Lily whom Blanche says gave her the strength to save her sister from the manipulative and brutal love of Stanley Kowalski.

BUNBURY: *Who's Afraid of Virginia Woolf?*

OLD ALGERNON: Of course! You've been feigning ignorance.

BUNBURY: No, just a guess, really. What of the mysterious woman who appears with him in *Virginia Woolf*?

OLD ALGERNON: She barely speaks. I think she has two lines.

BUNBURY: She's infinitely more important than you know. She's Rosaline.

OLD ALGERNON: Bunbury, this is the same argument we had seventy-five years ago. She never made it to the stage in Shakespeare's day—it's absurd to say she's significant in twentieth-century literature. What textual evidence do you have that this woman is Rosaline?

BUNBURY: Not textual, *actual. (Calling)* Hartley.

HARTLEY: *(Appearing)* Yes, sir.

BUNBURY: Please admit the young lady in Renaissance costume.

HARTLEY: Certainly, sir. *(Leaves)*

OLD ALGERNON: Good heavens, Bunbury. What are you doing?

BUNBURY: Proving to you that I'm no longer trivial, no longer simply smothered epigrams.

HARTLEY: *(Entering with* ROSALINE*)* The Lady Rosaline.

ROSALINE: Bunbury, what is this?

BUNBURY: Rosaline, this is Algernon. My own true love.

OLD ALGERNON: Bunbury! I beg your pardon!

ROSALINE: You love him still?

BUNBURY: I'm afraid I love him all the more. He's made a scholar of himself.

ROSALINE: *(Suspiciously)* A scholar? In what field? Not Renaissance, I hope?

(HARTLEY *has not left the room, and is in fact studying* ROSALINE *intently.*)

OLD ALGERNON: The lily motif in twentieth-century literature.

ROSALINE: You don't mean—?

BUNBURY: Yes!

OLD ALGERNON: The Man with the Lily, most specifically. What of it?

BUNBURY: He's been studying *me!*

ROSALINE: You are absurdly puffed up.

OLD ALGERNON: How in the world—? Bunbury, do you mean to say—?

BUNBURY: *(Producing the lily)* I'm the Man with the Lily!

OLD ALGERNON: Incredible!

ROSALINE: It's true, all right. He was there with that loathsome lily every time.

OLD ALGERNON: But in my research—I've just reached the conclusion—you'll be quite amazed—

OLD CECILY: *(Off)* Algy! Turn it on!

(OLD ALGERNON *winces, then gestures to* HARTLEY, *who turns on the television.*)

BUNBURY: Was that—?

OLD ALGERNON: *(Sighing)* Cecily. *(Shouting)* Yes, dear!

CECILY: *(Off.)* Are you coming down?

ROSALINE: *(Noticing the television)* What is that?

OLD ALGERNON: Surely you've seen a telly before.

(They look blank.)

OLD ALGERNON: A television. It shows you what's happening somewhere else.

CECILY: (Off) Algernon!

BUNBURY: What somewhere else?

VOICE OF NEIL ARMSTRONG: (On T V) That's one small step for a man—one giant leap for mankind.

OLD ALGERNON: (After a moment) The moon.

BUNBURY: The moon?!

ROSALINE: That man's on the moon?

OLD ALGERNON: Yes. As you can see, even Cecily is excited. She accuses me of ignoring the modern world, but it's not true. I remain optimistic. I see progress.

ROSALINE: (Staring at the T V, almost entranced) Technological progress, nothing else. More and more logic, less and less magic.

BUNBURY: She's a bit old-fashioned in her opinions, and alliterate to a fault.

OLD ALGERNON: Magic is indeed hard to come by. 'Tis difficult to find time to dream these days.

ROSALINE: Look at that funny suit!

BUNBURY: But you've been dreaming, Algernon! Speculating! Researching! What have you found?

OLD ALGERNON: God.

BUNBURY: Goodness, did you say God?

OLD ALGERNON: Yes, I've found God. It's clearly what he represents.

BUNBURY: What who represents?

OLD ALGERNON: The Man with the Lily. He's God. In Latin a *deus ex machina*, but a *deus* nonetheless. So you see, you're not in the least trivial.

BUNBURY: And yet I don't exist!

OLD ALGERNON: The very definition of God!
Who changes everything!

BUNBURY: Not everything. Only this handful of plays.
Certainly no effect on the real world, I've come to
realize.

OLD ALGERNON: You never know, my dear Bunbury.
You never know.

(HARTLEY *has been carefully edging closer and closer to*
ROSALINE. *She remains focused on the television.*)

ROSALINE: Quiet! Quiet, please! A handsome man is
speaking!

VOICE OF KENNEDY: *(On television, in a familiar Boston
accent)* For thousands of years, human beings have
gazed at the moon, loved it, feared it, worshipped it.
Today, we have touched it.

VOICE OF KENNEDY:	ROSALINE:
This is a bright day	Who is that man?
not just for America,	
but for the entire globe.	BUNBURY:
Now is the time for us	He seems important.
to join hands across	
the Earth and gaze	
into the future together.	OLD ALGERNON:
Competition led us to this	The American President.
day—the space race, we	
have called it. But we all	
have won this race—not	
just Americans, but all	
people, all nations have	
won this day. We are	HARTLEY:
transformed, transfigured,	Kennedy.
and stand in awe of what	
we have done. Nine years	
ago my brother held this	BUNBURY:
honored office and pledged	*What's* his name?

to you that we would send
a man to the moon.
With God's help,
with God's guidance, with   OLD ALGERNON:
God's gift of our ingenuity   Robert Kennedy.
and initiative, we have
done exactly that with
swiftness and assurance.

OLD CECILY: *(Off.)* Algernon, you're missing it!
You're missing everything!

*(HARTLEY has sidled up to ROSALINE and taken her hand.
She is only semi-conscious of his touch, but she accepts it
gratefully. At the same time, OLD ALGERNON and
BUNBURY have sat next to each other. BUNBURY puts his
arm around ALGERNON and ALGERNON puts his head
on BUNBURY's shoulder.)*

VOICE OF KENNEDY: But with my brother by my side,
I call for humbleness in achievement. I call for
generosity in spirit. It is often said the world is a terrible
place, and indeed there is hunger, war, and poverty
in every corner of the globe. Today the moon is our
inspiration for going forward, for changing our world,
for touching other worlds. Thank you, Jack, for leading
us to this day. And last of all, I call for peace. It can be
done. God bless us all.

END OF PLAY